Songbirds and Familiar Backyard Birds
Eastern Region

Text by Wayne R. Petersen

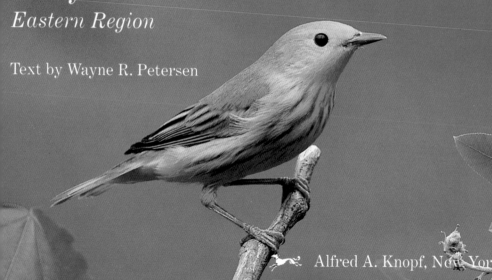

Alfred A. Knopf, New York

Contents

How to Use This Guide

Birds are among the most conspicuous and colorful of all wild creatures. Even in crowded cities and suburban parks, there is a surprising variety of bird species. Learning to identify birds is an enjoyable pursuit, an absorbing pastime that can last a lifetime.

Coverage

This handy guide provides information on 80 of the most common and frequently encountered birds in backyards and suburban areas of eastern North America. The majority of species are songbirds, but here also are other backyard birds such as doves and woodpeckers. The region covered by the book extends roughly from the Atlantic Ocean west to the foothills of the Rocky Mountains, north of Mexico. This traditional dividing line between eastern and western North America follows the 100th meridian, and marks a significant difference in habitats and species. The companion volume to western birds covers species west of this boundary.

Organization

The guide is divided into three parts: introductory information; illustrated species accounts; and appendices.

Introduction

This section of the guide provides tips on finding and seeing birds, information on identifying them, and a brief outline of the 30 bird families represented in this guide, and tips for attracting birds to your yard.

The Birds   The main part of this guide features color plates with accompanying text for 80 representative bird species. Important field marks, along with information about voice, habitat, and range, are described. There is also information on behavior, nesting habits, migration, and close relatives. An outline map showing nesting and winter ranges supplements the range statement in the text (see example at left). Where there is an overlap between nesting and winter ranges, or wherever a species occurs year-round, the crosshatching indicates the permanent range. For consistency, ranges are cut off at the Mexican border, even though many species occur south of there. Accompanying each species account is a small silhouette, designed as an aid in identification. These silhouettes represent general body types but do not necessarily indicate the subtle variations that can occur among species of the same family.

Breeding range

Winter range

Permanent range

Appendices   The labeled illustration in this section shows the major parts of a bird. The Glossary defines all the technical terms used in this book. Finally, the Index lists both scientific and common names of the species covered in this guide.

7

Birdwatching

Birdwatching is a fast-growing and enormously popular pastime. Estimates suggest between 60 and 80 million people are involved with birding to some extent. Many people are backyard birdwatchers who feed birds and in return enjoy watching a diversity of local birdlife throughout the year. At the other end of the spectrum are people whose birding interests take them to parks and wildlife refuges throughout the world. Many birders join organized bird walks, censusing projects, and fund-raising activities for conservation organizations. Typical of this group are the 42,000 birders who participate in over 2,000 National Audubon Society–Leica Christmas Bird Counts and National Audubon Society Birdathons, held annually across North America. Even more people enjoy birds as a complement to other activities, such as gardening, hiking, jogging, fishing, and boating.

Binoculars   A decent pair of binoculars can considerably enhance your enjoyment of birds. To be suitable for birding, binoculars should provide magnification of 7 to 10 power, have good optical clarity and light-gathering capability, and be easy to focus. Even beginning birders do well to invest in quality binoculars.

A few basic facts will get you started. Binocular specifications are stated as "# x #" (for example, 7 x 35). The first number refers to overall magnification; the second indicates the diameter in millimeters of the objective lens (the lens closest to the object you are observing). In this example, the binocular magnifies the image 7 times and has an objective lens that is 35 mm wide. If you divide the second number by the first, the result is what is called the "exit pupil," in this case, 5 because $35 \div 7 = 5$. This number gives a relative idea of how much light reaches the eye. A 10 x 40 binocular has an exit pupil of 4, which indicates that less light reaches the eye. But this is not the end of the story. Inexpensive binoculars might have a high exit pupil but poor optics; on the other hand, some fine binoculars have a relatively low exit pupil but provide a clear and bright image as a result of their exceptional optics and lens coating. Good binoculars generally combine high-quality optics with durable construction. Consider each of these factors when making a purchase. Binoculars range in price from $75 to $1,200. Very acceptable midrange binoculars, such as several Bausch and Lomb models endorsed by the National Audubon Society, may be bought for $200 to $500.

Spotting Scopes   For better views of birds such as waterfowl, hawks, and shorebirds, you may wish to invest in a spotting scope. Spotting scopes provide higher magnification than most binoculars, and because they are normally used on a tripod, they have the stability necessary for increased magnification. Prices and models vary and run from $200 to $700. The tripod is almost as significant as the telescope, and stability and portability are important qualities. An acceptable tripod will cost between $100 and $300.

When and Where to
Look for Birds   Birds can be found in a variety of habitats during all seasons. Winter offers a surprisingly good opportunity to see birds because many species come readily to suburban backyard feeders. In warmer weather, city parks, conservation lands, and open areas generally provide the habitat suitable for a wide variety of species to nest. During the migration seasons of spring and fall, birds can often be seen in atypical locations. Obviously, the greater the habitat diversification, the greater the number of species you are likely to encounter. With experience a birder develops a visual sense of the habitats preferred by different species, and then systematically visits as many of those habitats as possible. In general, areas with good cover and a source of

water are particularly attractive to many birds, although each species has its particular set of requirements.

Time of day and weather conditions also influence bird behavior. Sunny, calm conditions in early morning and late afternoon consistently produce the greatest bird activity, but even days with light showers can offer exciting birding possibilities. Windy weather is usually the least productive for bird finding.

Techniques for Finding Birds
There are many techniques for finding birds, and several deserve specific mention. First, move slowly and watch for even the slightest movement. When they are not singing, birds can be surprisingly inconspicuous, so pay attention to every chip note, leaf rustle, or moving twig. In open areas, look at dead snags for perched flycatchers or hawks, and regularly scan the sky for soaring birds or passing flocks. Where there are thickets or dense brush, make a sharp squeaking sound by kissing the back of the hand, or a hissing sound by vigorously saying "spish, spish, spish" to lure timid species into view. These sounds cause these birds to take a look at what they perceive to be a bird in distress. In forested areas, listen for chickadees because they often attract other small birds, especially during migration.

Identifying Birds

A helpful first step in making correct bird identifications is knowing what birds to expect in your area, as well as when and where to expect them. A state bird list, usually available from a local National Audubon Society chapter, can be particularly useful in this regard. By comparing the local or state bird list with the range descriptions in this guide, you can code the guide to indicate which species may be in your area in each season. Remember also that most of the birds in this book are likely to be encountered in suburban areas and backyards.

Size
The overall size of a bird can be critical to proper identification. Size is measured from the tip of the bill to the tip of the tail, and noted in the species accounts. By getting to know the sizes of common birds such as House Sparrow, American Robin, Rock Dove, and American Crow, you'll have a basis of comparison for judging the size of less familiar birds.

Shape
The silhouette and proportions of a bird are often sufficient clue to identifying the family a bird belongs to. When combined with the bird's actions and behavior, it is often possible to name the species as well. Note the bird's bill shape, tail proportions and shape, wing profile, and leg

length. Observe also such distinctive behavior as tail wagging, teetering, undulating flight, and feeding strategy.

Color and Pattern The colors and patterns of birds are usually what people notice first when they see an unfamiliar species. While color is critical for distinguishing certain species, color pattern can be equally useful. Look for precise color patterns and distinctive markings on key parts of the bird, then compare your observations with this guide's color illustrations and written descriptions. Refer to the glossary for an explanation of terms.

Voice Nearly all North American birds produce sounds, songs, and call notes that are specific to their species. Since voice can be helpful in locating and identifying birds, it is a good idea to learn to recognize bird songs and calls. While there are many things to consider when learning bird songs, three abilities are most important: the ability to hear bird sounds of differing frequency and pitch; to differentiate between sounds of similar frequency and pitch; and to recall a variety of bird sounds over an extended period of time. It is especially helpful to listen to bird song tapes or records that provide high-quality reproductions of actual bird songs and offer useful suggestions for learning the songs. With practice, you'll be able to use voice as an easy means of identifying birds.

Gestalt   Many birds can be identified by a composite impression that evolves from extensive experience with the species. Called "Gestalt" or "jizz," this is a birder's holistic impression of a species that combines shape, behavior, color, and pattern in ways that are often undefinable, yet allows an experienced observer to correctly identify a bird at great distance or under suboptimal conditions. For the beginner, however, it is necessary to be careful in observing and noting a bird's key features and behavior in order to identify the species.

How Birds Are Classified

Although all birds share certain fundamental character-istics, they are subdivided into distinct families and subfamilies. These groupings are based on structural characteristics, genetic similarity, vocalizations, and behavior. In this guide, 30 bird families and subfamilies are represented, some by only a single species. Knowing the characteristics of these groups is helpful in identifying an unfamiliar species. Just as the scientific names for birds are written in Latin, so too are the family and subfamily names. In the text that follows, these Latin names are in parentheses.

Hawks and Falcons

Hawks (Accipitridae) and falcons (Falconidae) are predatory birds with strong, hooked beaks, strong talons, and keen eyesight. They typically feed on small mammals, other birds, or large insects. Accipiters rely on stealth and surprise in order to capture small birds, while falcons prefer open country hunting where they use their slim, pointed wings to out-fly their prey or to hover in the open before dropping on an unsuspecting victim.

Quail

Quail (Phasianidae) are plump, chickenlike birds that spend most of their time walking on the ground scratching for seeds and insects. Many quail have loud and distinctive calls, and nearly all species are popular as gamebirds.

Pigeons and Doves Pigeons and doves (Columbidae) are round-bodied, small-headed, and fast-flying birds. Their cooing calls are occasionally mistaken for owls, and their feeding is usually done by walking slowly on the ground.

Cuckoos Cuckoos (Cuculidae) are slim, long-tailed, and reclusive. Although their call notes are often heard, they do not say "coo-koo" like the cuckoos of Europe.

Owls Owls (Strigidae) are predatory birds that generally hunt by night. With large, frontally placed eyes, hooked beaks, strong talons, and a soft plumage, they are able to capture a variety of small animals under the cover of darkness.

Nightjars Nightjars (Caprimulgidae) are a mysterious group of nocturnal birds that are often best known by their loud calls. With huge mouths and tiny beaks they fly about at night in pursuit of flying insects.

Swifts Swifts (Apodidae) are strong-flying, aerial feeders with sickle-shaped wings and tiny beaks. Their weak feet and stiff tails are adapted for vertically perching on cliff faces or the inside of chimneys.

Hummingbirds	Hummingbirds (Trochilidae) are tiny, long-billed, and energetic birds with iridescent plumage. They are able to hover in flight, and are most often observed feeding on the nectar of bright-colored flowers.
Woodpeckers	Woodpeckers (Picidae) are tree climbers that use their stiffened tails as props while they dig out insects and grubs from decaying tree bark with long, chisel-like beaks.
Flycatchers	Flycatchers (Tyrannidae) are big-headed, large-billed birds that capture flying insects by making periodic aerial sallies from a conspicuous perch. Many species are best identified by their distinctive call notes.
Swallows	Swallows (Hirundinidae) are aerial feeders that spend most of their time pursuing flying insects on the wing. Many species nest near human habitations and during migration; huge numbers may be seen together.
Jays and Crows	Jays and crows (Corvidae) are large, noisy, and intelligent, and are easily identified wherever they occur. Unlike many birds, they are practically omnivorous.
Chickadees and Titmice	Chickadees and titmice (Paridae) are small, gregarious, woodland birds that often visit birdfeeding stations. Their

confiding nature and winsome call notes generally make them popular species.

Nuthatches
Nuthatches (Sittidae) are small bark gleaners that are often seen clambering head-downward over the trunks and limbs of trees. They often associate with chickadees and titmice at birdfeeders.

Creepers
Creepers (Certhiidae) are tiny, inconspicuous birds that possess slender, decurved bills for extracting insects from bark crannies. They forage on tree trunks much like miniature woodpeckers.

Wrens
Wrens (Troglodytidae) are small, brown, and loud-singing birds that normally carry their stubby tails over their back. Many wrens readily nest in birdhouses.

Kinglets and Gnatcatchers
Kinglets and gnatcatchers (subfamily Sylviinae) and thrushes (subfamily Turdinae) all belong to the large family Muscicapidae. Diminutive and very active, kinglets are often found in association with chickadees or warblers. Gnatcatchers resemble slim, long-tailed warblers because of their energetic behavior and sharp, pointed bills. Thrushes, including the familiar robin, are fine songsters that prefer to dwell in forests where they feed on berries and insects.

Catbirds and Mockingbirds	Mimic-thrushes (Mimidae) such as catbirds and mockingbirds are slim and long-tailed and typically have complex songs that often incorporate imitations of other bird species. They often forage on the ground.
Waxwings	Waxwings (Bombycillidae) are gregarious wanderers that irregularly move about the countryside in search of fruiting berries. Colorful waxy tips on their secondaries (wing feathers) give them their name.
Starlings	Starlings (Sturnidae) are an Old World family that includes one introduced species that is now one of our commonest birds. Starlings are fine mimics of other birds' songs.
Vireos	Vireos (Vireonidae) are small woodland birds that resemble sluggish, thick-billed warblers. They may often be located in the forest canopy by listening for their persistent songs.
Emerizids	Emberizids (Emberizidae) are such a diverse group that they have no common name. Some of the more important subfamilies include the wood warblers (Parulinae), tanagers (Thraupinae), cardinals, grosbeaks, and buntings (Cardinalinae), towhees and sparrows (Emberizinae), and blackbirds (Icterinae). Wood warblers are small, brightly colored, and animated insect-eating birds whose variable

19

songs, spectacular migrations, and interesting behavior make them among the most popular group of birds in the New World. Tanagers are sluggish canopy dwellers whose bright colors and rich songs are reminiscent of the tropical forests where most members of this subfamily occur. Cardinals, buntings, grosbeaks, and sparrows are subfamilies that generally include talented songsters with thick, conical bills used for seed eating. Sparrows tend to be conservatively plumaged, while buntings and grosbeaks include some of North America's most colorful species. Blackbirds are generally black (although some have orange or yellow in their plumage), typically have sharp-pointed bills, and include many species that are beautiful songsters.

Finches Cardueline finches (Fringillidae), which are closely related to the emberizids, are brightly colored seed-eaters that readily visit backyard birdfeeders during the winter months.

Sparrows Weavers (Passeridae) are an Old World species that are represented in the United States by two introduced species.

Attracting Birds to Your Yard

There are various ways to attract birds to your yard. The most common are to plant trees, shrubs, and flowers that birds need for food or shelter; to dispense food or water; or to provide artificial nest boxes to attract cavity-nesting species. The setting and location of your property determines which of these techniques is most practical for your situation.

Planting for Birds

There are many ways to landscape for birds, but vegetation obviously determines which cover is especially crucial for nesting and for predator avoidance. By planting ground covers and low bushes beneath taller shrubs and trees, you can simulate the conditions of a natural woodland. If the trees and shrubs are selected carefully, the berries, fruits, and seeds they produce will attract birds. Try to select plants that produce seeds and fruit at different seasons of the year. There are also many flowers that are attractive to birds like hummingbirds, or that produce seeds relished by birds. Gardening books and magazine articles frequently describe the plant species most preferred by birds.

Feeders and Baths

Birdfeeders range from the simple to the elaborate. Plastic tube feeders typically dispense sunflower or thistle seed from small holes on the sides; chickadees, titmice, and small finches particularly like these feeders. Beef suet, relished by woodpeckers and nuthatches, can be put in coarsely knit bags of heavy twine and suspended from tree limbs. Mixed seed like cracked corn, millet, and sunflower seed can be thrown on the ground for ground feeders like doves, cardinals, and sparrows. In warm weather, feeders that hold sugar water often attract hummingbirds.

In all seasons, water is attractive to birds. In winter, electric coils or solar baths keep water from freezing, while in summer, dripping water is often more attractive than a well-stocked feeder.

Bird Boxes For cavity-nesting species, a suitable bird box often attracts birds to your yard. American Kestrels, Eastern Screech-Owls, Tree Swallows, chickadees, nuthatches, wrens, and Eastern Bluebirds all take readily to a properly constructed and located bird box. In some situations, competition from House Sparrows and European Starlings may pose a threat to these nesting species, but with persistence they can usually be discouraged. For several species, artificial nest boxes have proved to be a real benefit to survival, because natural tree cavities are becoming increasingly scarce.

Bird Conservation

Despite the great diversity of birds, many bird species are facing increasing threats to their populations. For example, in eastern North America, certain forest-breeding birds are affected by the continuous fragmentation of large, unbroken woodlands, which heightens the exposure of the nests to predators such as cats, dogs, raccoons, and skunks. Additionally, many species that winter in Latin America are losing their tropical habitats. The combined effect has been a loss in bird populations, reflected in long-term population studies such as the Breeding Bird Survey and the National Audubon Society–Leica Christmas Bird Count.

Controlling national and international events threatening native bird populations is possible through active support of conservation legislation and local wildlife management issues. BirdLife International is an organization with global concerns for declining bird populations. So is the National Audubon Society, whose "Birds in the Balance" program is working to halt the decline of some species by identifying critical migratory stopovers and breeding grounds in North America, and wintering areas in Central and South America. Supporting groups like these is a fine way to help the growing need for conservation.

The Birds

American Kestrel *Falco sparverius*

This smallest of North American raptors often perches on utility poles and roadside wires. Although American Kestrels occasionally capture small birds, they prefer mice and large insects, which they often hunt by hovering above the ground on rapidly beating wings. In spring and fall, large numbers may be encountered, particularly along coastal barrier islands, as they move to and from more northerly breeding sites. There appears to be recent evidence of a slow decline in the number of kestrels.

Identification 9–10½". A small bird with relatively long, pointed wings. The back and tail are rufous. Males have bluish-gray wings and a black band at end of the rusty tail; females have brown wings and a finely banded back and tail. Both sexes have 2 vertical black facial stripes.

Voice A shrill *killy killy killy.*

Habitat Open farmlands, fields, grasslands, woodland edges, and waste spots in urban areas.

Range Widespread across North America, except northern Alaska and northernmost Canada. Winters throughout most of U.S.

Northern Bobwhite *Colinus virginianus*

Popular as a game species, these small quail are often released where development, overhunting, or winter kill has reduced their numbers. As a result, many bobwhites in these areas are of a different genetic stock from that of ancestral populations. During the breeding season, Northern Bobwhites typically exist as isolated families. After nesting, families usually form coveys of up to 25 individuals that generally remain together throughout the winter.

Identification 8–11". A small, chickenlike bird, reddish brown above and white below with dark horizontal bars; the sides are streaked with chestnut. The throat and eyebrows are white in the male, buff in the female.

Voice Male gives a sharp, whistled *poor-bob-white* or *bob-white*, which rises at the end. Call note when the covey is separated is a whistled *whoil-ee*.

Habitat Farmlands, pastures, brushy areas, and pine barrens.

Range Resident from Nebraska, Iowa, and southern New England, south to Texas and Florida; also introduced in several western states.

Sharp-shinned Hawk *Accipiter striatus*

The Sharp-shinned Hawk (and larger and similar Cooper's Hawk) is a bird-hunting specialist. It often sits in the foliage of a tree watching for a suitable target. Having a long tail and short, rounded wings, this hawk flies stealthily through forested areas. During migration, thousands of these hawks may occasionally be seen passing over hawk-watching sites.

Identification 10–14". The adult is slaty above and on cap, barred rusty and whitish below; tail is banded with gray and dark brown and squarish or slightly notched. Females larger. Immatures are brown with a few irregular white spots above; underparts are whitish with brown streaks. Cooper's Hawk is larger (14–20"), tail rounded with prominent white terminal band; adult has dark cap contrasting with slaty back.

Voice Generally silent except near nest.

Habitat Forested areas; seacoasts, lakeshores, and mountain ridges during migration; suburban situations in winter.

Range Breeds from Alaska to Newfoundland, south to southern U.S. Winters from northern U.S. to Central America. Cooper's Hawk has a similar range but slightly more southern.

Rock Dove *Columba livia*

The Rock Dove, or "pigeon," was introduced to North America in the 17th century. Used as early as the days of the Roman Empire to carry messages over long distances, the bird has a remarkable homing ability, leading to experiments by animal behaviorists in an effort to discover how birds navigate. Although many questions still remain, it seems clear that pigeons use some combination of the angle of the sun in the sky, an internal clock, the earth's magnetic field, and possibly certain odors to help them fix their relative position and preferred direction of flight.

Identification	13". Typically blue-gray with a white rump and a dark terminal tail band. Iridescent green and purple on the neck are evident. Variations in color include brown, white, and pied forms.
Voice	A soft, mellow series of coos: *coo, coo, coo.*
Habitat	City streets, suburban parks, highway bridges, farmlands, and barns.
Range	Resident from southern Canada south to Mexico.

Mourning Dove *Zenaida macroura*

Although still protected in some states, in many areas the Mourning Dove is a popular and legally hunted game species. Originally a southern species, it now regularly occurs north to southern Canada. Its willingness to visit suburban birdfeeders has undoubtedly contributed to increased winter survival in the North. Mourning Doves are very prolific and often produce as many as five broods a year. Like most species of doves and pigeons, they feed their young a regurgitated food substance known as "pigeon milk." Adults feed primarily on seeds and grain. In winter, they roost in large aggregations, often in pine groves.

Identification | 11–13". Overall tan and buff with a long, pointed tail with white tips on outer tail feathers and black spots on wings.

Voice | A mournful cooing: *ooh-ee-ooh, woo, woo, woo.* Wings slap and whir during takeoff.

Habitat | Dry uplands, fields, parks, and suburban areas.

Range | Breeds from southern Canada south throughout the U.S. to Mexico. Regularly winters throughout the breeding range; also migrates south to Panama.

34

Common Ground-Dove *Columbina passerina*

In the Deep South and the Southwest, this smallest of North American doves is a common bird wherever an appropriate habitat exists. Its small size and confiding nature have saved it from becoming a popular game species, despite its abundance in some areas. Ground-doves are most often seen as they walk along roadside edges, their heads bobbing with every step, or in weedy fields, where they flush from nearly underfoot and fly away with rapid wing beats on a zigzag course.

Identification 6½–7". Grayish brown with black spots on the wings. The outer primaries are bright rufous in flight. The tail is stubby and rounded; its white corners are visible in flight.

Voice Call is a low, monotonous *woo-oo, woo-oo, woo-oo, woo-oo,* with each syllable rising at the end.

Habitat Open woodlands, pine flatwoods, fields, roadsides, sand dunes, and gardens.

Range Resident from southern California, central Arizona, and Texas to Florida, north along the coast to southeastern North Carolina; also south to South America.

Yellow-billed Cuckoo *Coccyzus americanus*

A slim, long-tailed skulker of thickets and second-growth woodlands, the Yellow-billed Cuckoo, like the similar Black-billed Cuckoo, is especially prevalent where there is a heavy infestation of caterpillars. Sometimes called a "rain crow," the cuckoo has a guttural call often heard just before or after a summer shower. Although Old World cuckoos are brood parasites—much like the Brown-headed Cowbird of North America—the Yellow-billed Cuckoo builds a flimsy stick nest of its own.

Identification 11–13". Gray-brown above, white below. The long tail shows large white spots below; primaries are rufous on top. The bill is slightly decurved, lower mandible yellow.

Voice Commonest call is a long, rapid, guttural *ka-ka-ka-ka-ka-ka-ka-ka-ka-kow-kow-kowlp-kowlp-kowlp-kowlp,* slower at end; also a hollow, slowly delivered *cowp, cowp, cowp, cowp.*

Habitat Woodlands, forest edges, thickets, and shade trees.

Range Breeds from southwestern British Columbia to Maine, but absent from northern Rockies and northern Great Plains, south to Mexico and Florida. Winters in South America.

Eastern Screech-Owl *Otus asio*

The Eastern Screech-Owl is undoubtedly one of the most common birds of prey in many parts of its range; however, its nocturnal behavior and habit of roosting in a tree cavity or dense thicket during the daytime often give little indication of its true abundance. Equally at home in a large birdhouse or a natural cavity, screech-owls frequently breed in residential areas and city parks, where only evening joggers and dog walkers are likely to hear their mournful, whinnying calls.

Identification 7–10". Two color phases: grayish and rufous; some birds intermediate. There are small, prominent ear tufts. Upperparts are mottled, with white spots on the wings; underparts are marked with dark streaks and bars.

Voice A long, tremulous, descending whinny; also a low, monotonous, rolled whistle. Easily imitated.

Habitat Deciduous woods, orchards, city parks, and well-planted suburban areas; often near streams or rivers.

Range Resident from southern Manitoba, southern Ontario, and New England, south to Texas and Florida.

Common Nighthawk *Chordeiles minor*

The Common Nighthawk, although not related to true hawks, is frequently noted "hawking" flying insects at twilight over cities and towns wherever there are flat-topped buildings for nesting. The nasal call notes and spectacular aerial courtship dives of males can be seen easily. In late summer, hundreds of nighthawks regularly congregate in river valleys and along lakeshores prior to migrating to South America. Nighthawks usually spend the day sleeping horizontally on a tree branch or on a flat roof.

Identification   9½–10". Mottled gray, white, black, and brown above; underparts buff, barred with brown with white throat patch. In flight, pointed wings show a white patch near the bend.

Voice   A nasal *beeerp,* given in flight. Male produces a loud whirring sound as air passes through the wings during courtship dives.

Habitat   Cities, pine barrens, open forests, and river valleys.

Range   Breeds from southeastern Alaska to Quebec, south to northern California, southeastern New Mexico, Texas, and Florida; more local in the West.

Chimney Swift *Chaetura pelagica*

In flight, the Chimney Swift's rapidly beating sickle-shaped wings give the illusion of alternate flapping, while its profile has been likened to a flying cigar. During migration, their arrival and departure often take place with great precision, as though the population migrated simultaneously. Swifts build shallow stick nests, which they paste together and fasten to the inside of chimneys with their own saliva. After breeding, the birds roost at night in large, abandoned chimneys. Owing to the weakness of their small feet, Chimney Swifts are unable to perch on branches.

Identification 5½". Uniformly sooty brown above, slightly paler below. The tail is short and stubby, the wings sickle-shaped. Often flies in early evening.

Voice A rapid twittering given in flight.

Habitat Urban and suburban areas, forest clearings, around old buildings, and any areas where abandoned chimneys exist.

Range Breeds from North Dakota to Maine, south to the Gulf Coast. Winters in South America.

Ruby-throated Hummingbird *Archilochus colubris*

The Ruby-throated is the only hummingbird that commonly occurs in eastern North America. Its tiny size, iridescent coloration, and remarkable flying ability make it almost unique among birds. On rapidly beating wings, it is often seen hovering in front of tubular flowers, where it obtains nectar and tiny insects with its needlelike bill. Despite its small size, the Ruby-throated flies twice annually across the Gulf of Mexico to and from its wintering grounds.

Identification 3¼–3½". A tiny bird with a needlelike bill. Upperparts are bright metallic green. The adult male is whitish below with grayish-olive flanks, an iridescent ruby-red throat (gorget) that may appear black in some light (the throat is whitish in immature males), and a dark tail. The female lacks the gorget and has white tips on the tail.

Voice A thin, squeaky *chick,* often run together as a series of *clicks.* Wings hum in flight.

Habitat Open woodlands, swampy thickets, gardens with flowers.

Range Breeds from central Alberta to Nova Scotia, south to eastern Texas, Florida. Winters in Mexico, Central America.

46

Red-headed Woodpecker *Melanerpes erythrocephalus*

The adult Red-headed Woodpecker is among the most striking birds in North America. It is frequently local in distribution and erratic near the fringes of its range. In winter, it caches acorns and beechnuts in bark crevices for later use. During summer, it often fly-catches from roadside fenceposts.

Identification	7½–9¼". The adult has a totally red head; the back, most of the wings, and the tail are glossy black. The wings have extensive white patches on trailing edge visible when bird is perched and in flight; underparts and rump are white.
Voice	Call is a loud *kweeer*, or *kwee-arr* uttered singly or in series; also various rattling and chattering notes.
Habitat	Open woodlands (especially oak and hickory), open areas with scattered large trees, city parks, edges of cornfields, and coastal areas during migration.
Range	Breeds from southeastern Alberta, southern Ontario, and southern New England, south to northeastern New Mexico, Texas, the Gulf Coast, and Florida. Winters irregularly north to Kansas and New Jersey.

Red-bellied Woodpecker *Melanerpes carolinus*

The Red-bellied Woodpecker is slowly expanding its range northward, especially in the Northeast. Its aggressive behavior and willingness to visit suburban birdfeeders have undoubtedly contributed to its success. Wherever they are found, Red-bellies inevitably betray their presence by their loud and frequently uttered call notes.

Identification 8½–9½". The adult male has black-and-white barred back and wings; the top of the head and nape are red, the cheeks and most of the underparts buff-white, and there is a reddish wash on the belly. The adult female is similar, except the forehead and crown are grayish white. In flight, both sexes show a white rump and band at the end of the wings.

Voice Common call is a loud *churr;* also a sustained, rattled *cha-aa-aa-aa.*

Habitat Deciduous and pine forests, parks, and residential areas.

Range Breeds from central South Dakota to Massachusetts, south to central Texas and Florida. Most northern birds move south in winter.

50

Yellow-bellied Sapsucker *Sphyrapicus varius*

The Yellow-bellied Sapsucker drills horizontal rows of small holes in the trunks of apple, cherry, and willow trees. The oozing sap and insects attracted by the sap are its favorite foods. Although generally quiet, the Yellow-bellied has a loud and distinctive drum often heard during breeding season.

Identification   7–8½". The upperparts are mottled and barred with black, white, and brown; the crown is red, with black-and-white stripes on the face. The rump is white, and wings show a white bar. The underparts are pale yellow, and there is a black crescent on the breast. The male's throat is red, female's is white. Immature birds have brownish heads.

Voice   Common note is a mewing *chur* or *quarr.* Drum is 2–3 rapid beats followed by series of double or triple beats.

Habitat   Northern hardwood and mixed forests; orchards, shade trees, and city parks during migration and winter.

Range   Breeds from Alaska and Newfoundland, south to British Columbia and Connecticut. Winters from Missouri and New Jersey south to Gulf Coast and Florida.

Downy Woodpecker *Picoides pubescens*

This species and the very similar, larger Hairy Woodpecker are widespread in North America. The Downy is our smallest woodpecker and is regularly found in woodlands, parks, and residential areas. Like all woodpeckers, the Downy has a chisel-like bill, an extra-long barbed tongue for extracting grubs from bark, and a proplike tail used for support as the bird hitches its way along tree trunks and limbs.

Identification 6–7". Black and white above, white below. The white cheeks are interrupted by a broad black line; a thin mustache runs from the bill to the back of the neck; black bars on the outer tail feathers. Hairy has a longer bill and pure white outer tail feathers. Males in both species have a red nape patch.

Voice Note is a dull *pik*; also a descending whinny: *dee-dee-dee-dee-dee*. The Hairy Woodpecker's note is sharper; also a loud rattle on one pitch.

Habitat Mixed woodlands, parks, and suburbs.

Range Resident throughout most of forested North America except in southwestern deserts.

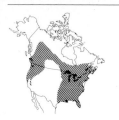

Pileated Woodpecker *Dryocopus pileatus*

A large and impressive species, the Pileated Woodpecker is encountered where large trees or extensive forest meets its rather precise requirements. Despite the Pileated's wary nature, its loud call and resonant drumming in early spring often betray its presence. Other signs are large oval excavations in dead or dying trees, where the birds seek beetle grubs beneath the bark. In southern states, the Pileated is more common in residential areas.

Identification 16½–19". A large bird, mainly black with black-and-white facial stripes, a white stripe on the side of the neck, white bases to the primaries, white wing linings, and a prominent red crown and crest (the male also has a red jaw stripe).

Voice Call is a loud, rolling *kuk-kuk-kuk-kuk-kuk-kuk,* often dropping in pitch at the end; variable.

Habitat Mature deciduous and mixed forests; large, forested suburban parks.

Range Resident from northern British Columbia, Ontario, and Quebec, south to northern California, Montana, eastern Nebraska, eastern Texas, the Gulf Coast, and Florida.

Northern Flicker *Colaptes auratus*

The "Yellow-shafted" Flicker of eastern North America and the "Red-shafted" and "Gilded" Flickers of western regions were once considered separate species. When ornithologists realized that the birds represented a single interbreeding population, the three entities were "lumped" into a single species. Northern Flickers are common and widespread across North America. Unlike most woodpeckers, flickers regularly forage on the ground for ants.

Identification 11–14". Brown with black barring above, heavily spotted with black below. Eastern males have a black mustache stripe; both sexes have a red nape patch and yellow underwings. In flight, the bold white rump patch is visible.

Voice A loud *wick-wick-wick-wick-wick!* Call notes include *wicka-wicka* and a loud, down-slurred *clear!*

Habitat Open woodlands, field edges, suburban areas, and coastal thickets during migration and winter.

Range Breeds virtually throughout North America south to Mexico; absent from southern Texas, except in winter. Found year-round in most of the U.S.

58

Eastern Wood-Pewee *Contopus virens*

Although the Eastern Wood-Pewee is nondescript in appearance, its plaintive call is one of the most pleasing among flycatchers. Most vocal at dawn and dusk, they also call throughout the day in dry deciduous forests and pine barrens, where they can be quite common. Like many flycatchers, wood-pewees are late migrants, often not appearing in northern states until the last half of May.

Identification   5–6". Call notes are diagnostic. The upperparts are olive-brown with two white wingbars, and there is no eye-ring; the underparts are whitish, often with a dusky wash across the breast. The Eastern Phoebe is similar but has a longer tail, lacks wingbars, and shows a contrast between the dark head and the lighter back.

Voice   Commonest call is a slow, mournful *pee-a-wee* (middle note lower), *peee-urr* (second note lower).

Habitat   Deciduous and mixed woodlands, and pine barrens.

Range   Breeds from southern Manitoba to Nova Scotia, south to eastern Texas, the Gulf Coast, and northern Florida. Winters in Central and South America.

Least Flycatcher *Empidonax minimus*

The Least is one of the most common of similar small flycatchers in eastern North America. The similarity among the species is so great that differences in habitat and call notes are often the only way to distinguish them in the field. Fortunately, the Least is quite vocal, often giving its snappy call many times in rapid succession. This is the latest of the small flycatchers to migrate in fall.

Identification   5¼". Best identified by habitat and voice. The upperparts are grayish olive; there are 2 white wingbars and a prominent eye-ring. The bill is short and triangular. The underparts are whitish.

Voice   Song is a sharp, repetitive *chebec, chebec,* with accent on the second syllable. Call note is a flat *wit.*

Habitat   Open deciduous forests, woodland clearings, groves, and farmyard shade trees.

Range   Breeds from the southern Yukon and southwestern Mackenzie to Nova Scotia, south to central Wyoming and New Jersey; also in mountains to northern Georgia. Winters from Mexico to South America.

Eastern Phoebe *Sayornis phoebe*

In northern states, the Eastern Phoebe is one of the earliest migrants to return in spring. Being typical flycatchers, phoebes sit on a conspicuous perch and sally out in pursuit of flying insects, then return and give a few lazy pumps of their tail. They often nest on the beams of porches or sheds, and regularly reuse the same nest. Phoebes are especially fond of fly-catching over streams and brooks.

Identification   6½–7". Grayish black above, darkest on the head, wings, and tail; lacks the eye-ring and wingbars of similar species. The underparts are whitish; the belly and flanks are lightly washed with yellow (especially immatures).

Voice   Song is a repeated *fee-bee, fee-bree,* with the second note higher or lower than the first. Call note is a sweet *chip.*

Habitat   Open woods, rocky cliffs, near streams and rivers with bridges, and residential areas suitable for nesting.

Range   Breeds east of the Rockies from southern Mackenzie and northern Saskatchewan east to New Brunswick, south to central Texas and Maryland. Winters from southern Oklahoma, the Gulf Coast, and Delaware south to Mexico.

64

Great Crested Flycatcher *Myiarchus crinitus*

Although this large flycatcher is quite common in many areas, it is often overlooked because it sits quietly in the canopy of trees. Unlike most flycatchers, Great Cresteds nest in tree cavities and have the curious habit of frequently incorporating a cast-off snake skin or piece of cellophane into their nest. This species regularly engages in noisy chase flights through the woods, with both other Great Cresteds and other species.

Identification 7–8". Olive-brown above with a pale gray throat and whitish wingbars. The belly is lemon-yellow; inner portions of the tail feathers and outer edges of the primaries are rufous.

Voice Song is a loud *wheerrup* or *whee-err*, often given at dawn. Call note is an emphatic *wheep*, sometimes repeated in stuttering fashion.

Habitat Deciduous and mixed forests, pine barrens, orchards, and suburban parks and woodlots.

Range Breeds from south-central Canada to New Brunswick, south to Texas, the Gulf Coast, and Florida. Winters in southern Florida, Mexico, and South America.

Eastern Kingbird *Tyrannus tyrannus*

The Eastern Kingbird is conspicuous because of its habit of sitting on wires and fences, its bickering calls, and its belligerent behavior. Seemingly afraid of nothing, kingbirds are often seen in pursuit of hawks, crows, and grackles—in fact, almost any bird that passes too close to their perch. In late summer, dozens of Eastern Kingbirds can be seen congregating on roadside phone wires and in outer coastal thickets prior to fall migration. During nesting season, kingbirds are rather solitary and feed exclusively on insects.

Identification	8½–9". The head and upperparts are dark bluish-black; the underparts are white. There is a distinct white terminal band on the tail.
Voice	A stuttering *kip-kip-kipper-kipper*; also a buzzy *dzeet*.
Habitat	Woodland edges, streamsides, country roadsides, and farmlands; coastal thickets during migration.
Range	Breeds from northern British Columbia east to the Canadian Maritime Provinces, south to northern California, central Texas, the Gulf Coast, and Florida. Winters in South America.

Scissor-tailed Flycatcher *Tyrannus forficatus*

The Scissor-tailed Flycatcher is both conspicuous and elegant as it perches on roadside fences and phone wires in open country. It often drops to the ground to capture insects rather than snapping them out of the air. During courtship, it makes spectacular aerial displays that typically include high, spiraling flights followed by downward-dashing plunges, frequently punctuated by dramatic reverse somersaults.

Identification 12–15". The upperparts are pale gray; wings are black. The underparts are gray with a pinkish wash on the sides; underwings are bright pinkish orange. The tail is very long, deeply forked, and patterned with black and white. Females are paler and shorter-tailed than males.

Voice Various chattering and spluttering notes; also a hard *kip*.

Habitat Open plains, farmlands, and roadside fences.

Range Breeds from southern Nebraska and southern Colorado south to western and southern Texas and western Louisiana. Winters in Mexico and Central America; small numbers in southern Florida.

70

Purple Martin *Progne subis*

This largest of North American swallows is one of few colonial breeders that take readily to apartment-style nesting. Ancestrally, martins were cavity nesters; however, today most colonies are in bird boxes containing up to 100 compartments. Purple Martins subsist exclusively on flying insects and are vulnerable to the effects of prolonged late-spring rains and cool weather. Martins are frequently difficult to attract to new colony sites, although their fidelity to established sites is remarkable.

Identification 7–8". The adult male is glossy blue above and below; its tail is rather long and prominently notched. Females and immature males are duller above and pale gray below.

Voice A series of rich, gurgled notes; also a single or double *tyu* given in flight.

Habitat Open woodlands and farmlands; often near ponds or lakes.

Range Breeds from Alberta east across southern Canada to Nova Scotia, south to New Mexico, Texas, and Florida; also along the Pacific coast from southern British Columbia to southern California. Winters in South America.

72

Tree Swallow *Tachycineta bicolor*

Whereas Tree Swallows normally nest in tree cavities, they readily take to appropriately constructed birdhouses. They build their nests out of grass and feathers, but often have their eggs or young destroyed by competing House Sparrows or European Starlings. Prior to migration in late summer and fall, tremendous swarms of Tree Swallows gather in coastal areas, where they feed on bayberries and insects. At night, flocks roost in marshes or tall grasses.

Identification	5–6". Males are blue or blue-green above and pure white below; females and immatures are duller, grayish brown above; juveniles often have a slight suggestion of a partial collar across the breast.
Voice	Song is a soft, liquid warble; also a twittering *tsweet tsweet.*
Habitat	Open wetlands, beaver ponds, orchards, field edges, and unforested suburban areas; seashores during migration.
Range	Breeds from Alaska to Labrador south to southern California and Maryland, occasionally to the Gulf Coast. Winters from central California and the Gulf states south to Central America; casually north to New York.

74

Barn Swallow *Hirundo rustica*

A streamlined aerialist, the Barn Swallow is found worldwide, with some individuals annually migrating as far south as Tierra del Fuego. Because of the affinity of these birds for barns, warehouses, and bridges as nesting sites, it is easy to observe their curious behavior, in which several Barn Swallows alternately drop and catch a windborne feather. Barn Swallows frequently forage over grassy fields, especially when mowing disturbs flying insects.

Identification 6¾–7¾". The upperparts are steely blue, with rusty or buff underparts (palest in females); the forehead and throat are chestnut. The tail is long, pointed, and deeply forked, with white spots near the base.

Voice Most often a sustained series of chattering and twittering notes; also a soft *wit* and a clear *slip* given in flight.

Habitat Open areas, farmlands, marshes, lakeshores, and suburbs.

Range Breeds from Alaska and northern Alberta east to Newfoundland and south throughout most of the U.S.; absent from the Gulf Coast and parts of the interior Gulf states. Winters in Central and South America.

Blue Jay *Cyanocitta cristata*

The Blue Jay is among the most flamboyant and behaviorally interesting birds in eastern North America. Its remarkably varied vocalizations, conspicuous diurnal migrations, and tendency to visit birdfeeders in winter make it visible and familiar to most people. Unfortunately, its habit of robbing the eggs and young of other songbirds sometimes taints its popularity. On the plus side, it consumes quantities of insects, including forest pests such as gypsy moth caterpillars.

Identification 11½–12½". A large bird, bright blue above, with a blue crest, black-and-white spots on the wings, and black facial markings. The underparts are grayish white with a black necklace; the tail has a white tip.

Voice Most common calls are a harsh *jay-jay* and *thief-thief*; also *queedle, queedle* and a hoarse, dry rattle.

Habitat Widespread; deciduous and mixed forests, parks, suburbs.

Range Central Alberta to Newfoundland, south to eastern New Mexico, southeastern Texas, the Gulf Coast, and southern Florida. Northern birds usually move south in winter.

American Crow *Corvus brachyrhynchos*

The American Crow's distinctive and diverse vocalizations and its conspicuous presence make it one of our most familiar bird species. In the Southeast, the species often overlaps with the slightly smaller and more nasal-voiced Fish Crow. In spite of bounties and indiscriminate hunting, the American Crow has prevailed, and today winter roosts often number in the tens of thousands.

Identification 17–21". A large bird, uniformly glossy black. Fish Crow is best distinguished from American Crow by its more nasal call, range, and preference for tidewater areas.

Voice Most familiar call is a loud and raucous *caw caw caw!*; other sounds include a dry rattle and various guttural croaks.

Habitat Farmlands, woodlands, suburbs, city parks, and seashores.

Range Breeds throughout the southern two-thirds of Canada and most of the U.S.; absent from much of the interior Southwest. Winters south of the Canadian border. Fish Crow is resident from southern New England south along the coast to Florida, the Gulf Coast, and extreme eastern Texas; also Mississippi drainage north to southern Illinois.

80

Black-capped Chickadee *Parus atricapillus*

The Black-capped Chickadee is among the favorite birds of many birdwatchers. Its small size, acrobatic behavior, and confiding nature contribute to its popularity, as does the frequency with which it uses birdfeeders and birdhouses. Occasionally they undergo substantial fall migrations because of food scarcity or population pressures.

Identification 5¾". In the eastern U.S., the Black-capped and Carolina chickadees are nearly identical, with primarily voice and range differences. Both are small, gray above and whitish below, with buff or light rusty flanks, black cap and bib, and white cheeks. Carolina looks bigger-headed and shorter-tailed with a more defined lower edge to the black bib.

Voice Song of the Black-capped is a clear, whistled *fee-bee,* with first note higher; Carolina whistles a 4-note *fee-bee, fee-bay.* Call is a clear *chick-a-dee-dee-dee,* faster in the Carolina.

Habitat Mixed forests; residential areas, especially in winter.

Range The Black-capped is resident from Alaska to Newfoundland, south to California and northern New Jersey; Carolina is from Kansas and New Jersey south to Texas and Florida.

Tufted Titmouse *Parus bicolor*

The Tufted Titmouse is a common resident of deciduous woodlands in much of the eastern United States. Its willingness to visit birdfeeders and to associate with chickadees, nuthatches, and Downy Woodpeckers makes it especially popular. In spring, its loud whistled calls make it particularly conspicuous; by early summer, it becomes silent and rather reclusive while nesting. Prior to 1960, on the Atlantic Coast it bred only as far north as southern Connecticut, but today it is an established resident from southern Minnesota to Maine.

Identification	4½–6½". Gray above; grayish white below with reddish-buff flanks. There is a conspicuous dark gray crest (black in the Texas population).
Voice	Song is a loud, whistled *peter-peter-peter;* also buzzy or grating scold notes and a high *seea, seea* during courtship.
Habitat	Deciduous and mixed forests, brushy swamps, residential parks, and suburban areas (especially in winter).
Range	Resident from Nebraska and southern Michigan to Maine, south to Mexico and central Florida.

Red-breasted Nuthatch *Sitta canadensis*

The Red-breasted Nuthatch is a denizen of coniferous forests, where it is often seen investigating dense clusters of evergreen needles and cones for small insect larvae and conifer seeds. Its small size, stubby tail, jerky flight, and nasal call notes are often the best clues to its identity as it moves about high overhead. They regularly visit feeders in winter.

Identification 4½–4¾". The upperparts are bluish gray; the crown is black in males, gray in females. There is a bold white eyebrow stripe. The underparts are rusty or buff-brown.

Voice Common call is a slow, nasal *nyak nyak;* also a rapid series of nasal notes when agitated.

Habitat Coniferous forests; mixed forests and suburban areas during migration and winter.

Range Widespread resident in many parts of Canada and the U.S. In the East, breeds from the Great Lakes and Newfoundland south in the Appalachians to North Carolina, as well as along the northeast coast.

White-breasted Nuthatch *Sitta carolinensis*

The White-breasted Nuthatch is common and widespread across much of North America and is regularly found at birdfeeders along with chickadees, titmice, and Downy Woodpeckers. Like all nuthatches, this species characteristically forages for tiny insects and their larvae by creeping head-downward along the limbs and trunks of forest trees. The common name derives from its habit of "hatching," or hacking open, small seeds that also constitute part of its diet. White-breasted Nuthatches nest in tree cavities, where they lay as many as eight to ten eggs.

Identification   5–6". Gray above and white below, with a black cap and nape and rusty undertail coverts. White spots in the tail corners are visible in flight.

Voice   Call note is a nasal *yank yank;* in spring, a rapid *to-what what what what.*

Habitat   Deciduous and mixed woodlands, parks, and suburban areas.

Range   Resident in most of southern Canada and throughout most of the U.S. except the Great Plains.

Brown Creeper *Certhia americana*

Like a miniature woodpecker, this tiny and unobtrusive bird methodically hitches its way up tree trunks as it explores every nook and cranny for food. At night, occasionally several creepers will gather to form a tiny, circular rosette on the side of a tree, presumably to share body heat on cold evenings. Unlike woodpeckers, Brown Creepers build their nests behind loose pieces of tree bark.

Identification   5–5½". The head and upperparts are brown, streaked with grayish white. The underparts are whitish, tinged with buff on flanks and undertail coverts. Decurved bill is thin.

Voice   Song is a thin, wiry *see-tee-wee-tu-wee;* given in early spring. Call note is a single, high, thin *seep.*

Habitat   Cool, rich, coniferous or mixed woodlands; swampy woods; and parks and coastal areas during migration.

Range   Breeds from southeastern Alaska to Newfoundland, south in western mountains to Central America; southern Wisconsin east to New England, south in the Appalachians to western North Carolina. Winters south to the Gulf Coast and central Florida.

Carolina Wren *Thryothorus ludovicianus*

The Carolina Wren is the largest and one of the most familiar of eastern wrens. As at home nesting in a little-used watering can, clothespin bag, or mailbox as in a birdhouse or natural cavity, this bird has a curious nature and a loud, ringing song. While especially abundant in the South, increasingly it is found well into New England, where, historically, it was subject to severe winter mortality. Undoubtedly, mild winters and backyard birdfeeding are enhancing its winter survival in that region.

Identification 5½–6". The upperparts are a rich rufous, with dark barring on the wings and tail; the underparts are bright buff. Long, slender bill and broad, white eyebrow stripe are distinctive.

Voice Song is clear, loud, and ringing, usually 3-syllabled and repeated 3–5 times: *wheedle, wheedle, wheedle* or *tea-kettle, tea-kettle, tea-kettle.* Other sounds include a descending *teeer* and a variety of buzzy scold notes.

Habitat Bushy tangles, thickets, forest undergrowth, and shrubbery.

Range Resident from southern Iowa to New England, south to central Texas and Florida.

92

House Wren *Troglodytes aedon*

Like most bird species, the House Wren establishes and defends a nesting territory. Indeed, the cheerful, babbling song of the male is often delivered many times in succession throughout the day. But even though the House Wren's territory is small, both male and female aggressively defend and drive away other House Wrens. They will also destroy the nests and eggs of competing pairs or sometimes other species.

Identification 4½–5". Overall a rather plain bird, brownish gray above and buff below. There is a faint eyestripe and light barring on the wings and tail; the tail is often cocked over the back.

Voice An exuberant, cascading series of bubbling notes. Scold note is a grating, sizzling sound.

Habitat Brushy areas, woodland edges, orchards, and suburban yards.

Range Breeds from southern Canada throughout the U.S., except in the extreme Southeast. Winters from southern California and Virginia southward.

Golden-crowned Kinglet *Regulus satrapa*

Kinglets are nervous little birds that characteristically inhabit dense coniferous forests, where their high, lisping call notes are often the best indication of their presence. Their incessant wing-flicking and their habit of hovering at the tip of a branch as they forage for insects are quite diagnostic.

Identification 4". A very tiny bird, olive above with white wingbars and eyebrows; grayish white below. The crown is orange-yellow in males, yellow in females, and bordered in black.

Voice Song is a very high-pitched, ascending series of *see see see see* notes, dropping abruptly in a rapid chatter at the end. Call note is a high, trebled *see-see-see*.

Habitat Coniferous forests in summer; other woodlands, including suburban areas, during migration and winter.

Range Breeds from Alaska to Newfoundland, south in suitable coniferous forests in California, Colorado, Minnesota, and the southern Appalachians; absent from the Great Plains and most of the Southeast. Winters from southern Canada throughout most of U.S.

96

Ruby-crowned Kinglet *Regulus calendula*

Owing to their small size and high metabolism, kinglets are constantly foraging for food, usually with great energy and apparent nervousness. Because they are so tiny, they seem to be periodically subject to severe winter mortality. Unlike the closely related Golden-crowned Kinglet, the Ruby-crowned has a remarkably loud and variable whistled song. It is one of the first migrant songbirds heard in spring.

Identification 4¼". The upperparts are olive-gray, the underparts whitish buff. There is a white eye-ring and 2 white wingbars (the leading one is often concealed). The male's red crown patch is often concealed.

Voice Song is a loud and variable *tee tee, tew tew tew, teedadee teedadee teedadee teedadee.* Call note is a husky *did-it.*

Habitat Coniferous forests in summer; other woodlands and suburban areas during migration and winter.

Range Breeds from northwestern Alaska and Newfoundland, south in mountains to Lower California, New Mexico, the Great Lakes region, and northern New England. Winters from British Columbia, northern Texas, and Maryland south.

98

Blue-gray Gnatcatcher *Polioptila caerulea*

A slim, tiny, animated inhabitant of trees and shrubbery, this bird's thin, squeaky call notes are the best indication of its presence, since its small size and constant activity make it difficult to locate. As it moves about looking for tiny insects, it has a habit of twitching, fanning, or cocking its long, slender tail. The nest of the Blue-gray Gnatcatcher is usually high on a horizontal branch, decorated with lichen.

Identification   4½–5". A tiny and slim bird with bluish-gray upperparts, darker wings, and white eye-ring. Underparts are whitish; tail is black above, white below, with white outer feathers.

Voice   Song is a short, thin, squeaky series of notes, usually including a few warbled phrases. Call note is a high, wheezy *psee, tsee,* or *zhee.*

Habitat   Open woodlands, dense shrubbery, trees along rivers, and suburban parks.

Range   Breeds from northern California east across the Great Plains to the Great Lakes region and southern Maine, south to northern Central America. Winters from the southern states south to Mexico.

100

Eastern Bluebird *Sialia sialis*

Bluebirds were among the songbirds hardest hit during the period of DDT overuse, and they have also continually had to compete for nesting space with alien cavity-nesting species such as European Starlings and House Sparrows. Additionally, as agriculture has declined in the Northeast, suitable habitat has also disappeared. Despite these setbacks, the soft, liquid warble of the bluebird's song is increasingly heard as the birds respond to intensive nest-box erection on their behalf.

Identification	6–6½". The male is bright blue above with a rusty throat and breast and a white belly. The female is similar but duller. Juveniles are dull, lightly spotted above and below.
Voice	Song is a soft, rich warble. Call note is a liquid *chur-lee,* often given in flight.
Habitat	Farmlands, orchards, open forests, and burned woodlands.
Range	Breeds from southern Saskatchewan to southern Quebec and the Maritime Provinces, south to eastern New Mexico, the Gulf Coast, and Florida. Winters in southern parts of its breeding range south to Nicaragua.

Wood Thrush *Hylocichla mustelina*

In the eastern United States, few sounds have the rich, flutelike harmonics of the Wood Thrush's song. A look at the large, dark eyes of a Wood Thrush reveals the species' fondness for shade, and it is no surprise that much of its singing is at dawn and dusk. Primarily a species of extensive and interior forests, in patchy woodlands Wood Thrushes are becoming increasingly vulnerable to the brood-parasitic Brown-headed Cowbird, which flourishes in these fragmented areas.

Identification   7½–8½". The upperparts are cinnamon-rufous, brightest on the head and nape. It is white below with extensive, large, round black spots. Juveniles are lightly spotted with gray on the head and upperparts.

Voice   Song is a short, flutelike, 3-syllable *ee-o-lay*. Call note is a sharp, emphatic *pip-pip-pip,* often given at dusk.

Habitat   Deciduous and mixed woodlands, moist thickets, and suburban areas with dense cover.

Range   Breeds from Ontario to Nova Scotia, south to the Gulf Coast and Mexico. Winters in Mexico and Central America.

104

American Robin *Turdus migratorius*

The American Robin is perhaps one of North America's best-known songbirds, whose spring caroling is often perceived as a sign of the season. Actually, large numbers of robins routinely winter in the northern states, where they feed on fruits and berries by day and gather into sizable evening roosts. The robin is also famous as an earthworm hunter—a prey it locates visually. Because the bird normally incorporates a layer of mud into its nest, the nest is easily found after the leaves are off the trees.

Identification 9–11". The upperparts are gray-brown; the underparts are rusty orange. There are white crescents around the eye, a yellow bill, and a white-striped throat.

Voice Song rises and falls and has a caroling quality: *cheerily-cheer-up! cheerily-cheer-up!* Call notes include a descending whinny, a low *chuck,* and *tut, tut.*

Habitat Woodlands and suburban areas; wet plowed fields during migration.

Range Breeds throughout most of North America south to Mexico. Winters mainly in the southern two-thirds of U.S.

Gray Catbird *Dumetella carolinensis*

This saucy and vociferous mimic is as at home in suburban shrubbery as in the dense undergrowth of swampy woodlands. In late summer, catbirds fairly throng in coastal thickets or moist tangles where there is an abundance of berries to eat. Their catlike mewing and petulant scold notes are a common sound, and making a sharp kissing sound on your hand will invariably draw several in for a closer look. When singing, catbirds seldom repeat phrases the way thrashers and mockingbirds tend to do.

Identification	9". A slim, long-tailed bird, uniformly dark gray with a black cap and rusty undertail coverts.
Voice	Song is a disjointed jumble of notes, interspersed with pauses, catlike mews, and various imitations. Commonest call is a catlike scold; also a harsh *tcheek-tcheek*.
Habitat	Moist thickets, undergrowth, suburban shrubbery.
Range	Breeds from British Columbia to Nova Scotia, south to eastern Oregon, central Arizona, northern Texas, and central Georgia. Winters along the mid-Atlantic and Gulf coasts, south to Central America.

Northern Mockingbird *Mimus polyglottos*

Anyone with a mockingbird in the neighborhood is sure to know about it. One of North America's most gifted mimics, the Northern Mockingbird loudly proclaims its territory day and night with an extraordinary variety of sounds and imitations of other birds in the area. Apparently, the most reproductively successful males have the most extensive repertoire of vocalizations. Unlike many species, "mockers" defend a winter feeding territory as well as a breeding territory, and are often seen in chase flights at any season.

Identification 9–11". Gray above and dirty white below, with 2 white wingbars and a white patch on the wing in flight; the outer tail feathers are white. Often perches on wires and poles.

Voice An emphatic and tireless singer, it mimics the songs of other birds, repeating phrases usually 3 or more times. Call note is a harsh *tchak*.

Habitat Brushy fields, woodland edges, scrub, thickets, and suburban areas.

Range More or less resident from California, Wisconsin, and Nova Scotia south to Mexico and Florida.

Brown Thrasher *Toxostoma rufum*

The slim, long-tailed Brown Thrasher is a rather reclusive inhabitant of brushy second growth and forest edges. Its loud and complex song is frequently the best indication of its presence. Mounted atop a tall tree or bush in early morning or late afternoon, the bird puts forth paired phrases of melodious song, which readily distinguish it from the more repetitive song of the Northern Mockingbird.

Identification 11½". A long-tailed bird with rufous upperparts and 2 white wingbars. The underparts are whitish, washed with buff and heavily streaked with dark brown.

Voice Song is a continuous, musical blend of varied phrases, each repeated twice. Call note is a dull *smack;* also a distinctive crackling sound.

Habitat Brushy fields, woodland edges, hedgerows, thickets, pine barrens, and suburban gardens.

Range Breeds from Manitoba to Maine, south to eastern Texas, the Gulf Coast, and southern Florida. Winters in the Southeast and eastern Texas, north along the Atlantic coast to Massachusetts.

Cedar Waxwing *Bombycilla cedrorum*

The Cedar Waxwing derives its common name from its preference for cedar berries and from the waxy red tips on its secondary wing feathers. The bird is a gregarious wanderer whose movements, especially in winter, are governed by concentrations of small fruits and berries produced in variable abundance from year to year. In summer, it also feeds like a flycatcher on flying insects. Cedar Waxwings have very small territories, which often results in nests that are remarkably close together.

Identification   7¼–8". The upperparts and breast are warm brown; the belly is yellowish. The black face mask, crested head, and yellow terminal band on the gray tail are most distinctive; there are red tips to the secondaries. Juveniles are duller.

Voice   A high, lisping *ssseee* or *tseee tseee tseee.*

Habitat   Residential areas, roadsides, woodland edges, and orchards; usually near berries or fruit trees.

Range   Breeds from southern Alaska to Newfoundland, south to northern California, Virginia, and in mountains to Georgia. Winters throughout most of U.S.

114

European Starling *Sturnus vulgaris*

For the urban birdwatcher, the aerial gyrations at twilight of European Starlings going to roost beneath traffic-crowded bridges provide one of the daily pleasures of city living. In addition, the birds are skillful mimics and have a number of engaging behaviors that are readily observed. Unfortunately, since their introduction into the United States from Europe in 1890, they have become serious city and agricultural pests, and their cavity-nesting behavior is frequently at the expense of native hole-nesting species.

Identification 7½–8½". A chunky bird with a short, square tail. In spring, it is black with an iridescent blue and green gloss; the bill is yellow. Winter plumage is heavily speckled with white; the bill is dark. Juveniles are dusky gray.

Voice A remarkable variety of chatters, squeaks, clicks, and whistles; often gives a "wolf whistle," as well as mimicking other birds.

Habitat Cities, parks, roadsides, coastal salt marshes, and farmlands.

Range Throughout the U.S. and southern Canada.

116

Warbling Vireo *Vireo gilvus*

The Warbling Vireo is among the most nondescript birds in North America. Fortunately, its whereabouts is frequently betrayed by its husky, rambling song, often given in rapid succession. A widespread species, Warbling Vireos occupy a variety of habitats. Like most vireo species, they build beautifully constructed cup nests in the horizontal forks of branches. Males often sing while incubating.

Identification 5–6". The upperparts are light olive-gray; the eyebrow is whitish. The underparts are whitish, occasionally tinged yellowish on sides and flanks (especially immatures in fall).

Voice Song is a husky, continuous warble, often ending abruptly on a rising note. Call note is a wheezy, querulous *tshay, tshay.*

Habitat Tall streamside trees, aspen groves, open woodlands, roadside shade trees, and suburban parks.

Range Breeds from northern British Columbia across southern Canada to southern New Brunswick, south to Mexico, northern Alabama, and Virginia. Winters in Mexico and Central America.

Red-eyed Vireo *Vireo olivaceus*

Although once one of the most common songbirds in North America, the Red-eyed Vireo is now declining, suffering from forest fragmentation, increasing nest parasitism by Brown-headed Cowbirds, and destruction of habitat in its tropical wintering areas. This is one of few forest birds to regularly sing in the heat of a midsummer day.

Identification	5½–6½". The upperparts, wings, and tail are olive-green; underparts are whitish, with a yellowish wash on the flanks. The crown is gray, bordered with black. There are white eyebrows and a dark eye-line; eyes are red in adults.
Voice	Song is a continuous, repetitive series of short, robinlike phrases, usually given with rising and falling inflection. Call note is a harsh *where?*
Habitat	Deciduous and mixed forests, parks, and residential areas.
Range	Breeds from northern British Columbia across southern Canada to Nova Scotia, south to Oregon, Colorado, central Texas, the Gulf Coast, and central Florida. Winters in South America.

120

Yellow Warbler *Dendroica petechia*

This common species is found throughout most of North America from spring to fall. Although the bird's sprightly song is one of the earliest of wood warblers' songs to be heard in spring, this is one of the first species to depart southward after nesting. Yellow Warblers are a favorite host of the brood-parasitic Brown-headed Cowbird, however upon the appearance of a cowbird egg in their nest, they build a new nest atop the old, occasionally up to six times if need be.

Identification | 4½–5". Bright yellow below, greenish yellow above. The male has thin chestnut streaks on the underparts; both sexes have yellow patches in the outer tail feathers. Immatures in fall are a rather uniform yellowish green.

Voice | Song is a cheerful, *sweet,* and rapid *sweet-sweet-sweet, sitta, sitta, see.* Call note is a sharp *chip.*

Habitat | Streamside thickets, bushy wet meadows, swampy areas, willow and alder thickets, and gardens.

Range | Breeds from Alaska through most of Canada and the U.S. Winters in the tropics.

122

Pine Warbler *Dendroica pinus*

The Pine Warbler occurs nearly everywhere in the eastern United States where there is extensive growth of mature pine trees. Pine Warblers so prefer pines that even in mixed forest situations, the birds seldom venture far from the dense needles that they favor. In the southern parts of their range, Pine Warblers remain throughout the year.

Identification 5–5½". Adults are unstreaked olive-green above, with white wingbars and tail spots. The underparts are yellow with indistinct dark streaks on the breast and sides; undertail coverts are white.

Voice Song is a musical trill, usually on the same pitch; similar to the Chipping Sparrow's but slower and sweeter.

Habitat Mature pine forests, pine barrens, pine flatwoods, and isolated pine groves in mixed forests.

Range Breeds from southeastern Manitoba to central Maine, south to eastern Texas and Florida; rare in the Mississippi and Ohio river valleys. Winters from southern Illinois and New Jersey, occasionally north along the coast to Massachusetts, south to southern Florida, the Gulf Coast, and Texas.

124

Yellow-rumped Warbler *Dendroica coronata*

The widespread and geographically variable Yellow-rumped Warbler was formerly called the "Myrtle" in the East and "Audubon's" in the West. Yellow-rumpeds regularly winter on the Atlantic coast as far north as New England. Often abundant during fall migration and winter, especially in coastal thickets, they eat bayberries and wax myrtle.

Identification 5–6". The breeding male "Myrtle" is blue-gray above with dark back streaks; the small crown patch and rump are bright yellow. The underparts and throat are white; the chest, sides, and flanks are heavily marked with black streaks, and there is a yellow patch at the side of the upper breast and white spots in the tail corners.

Voice Song is a colorless trill: *tuwee-tuwee-tuwee-tuwee,* usually dropping in pitch at the end. Call note is a sharp *check*.

Habitat Coniferous and mixed forests; city parks, residential areas, and coastal thickets during migration.

Range "Myrtle" form breeds from Alaska to Newfoundland, south through most of Canada and New England. Winters chiefly in the Southeast.

American Redstart *Setophaga ruticilla*

Animated and colorful, the American Redstart obtains food by making active sallies after flying insects. The bright squares of orange or yellow are conspicuous as the birds fan their tails and droop their wings while foraging. Unlike most warblers, male Redstarts in their first spring maintain a plumage similar to that of females.

Identification   4½–5½". The adult male is glossy black on the head, back, and breast; there are bright orange patches on the wings, tail, and sides of the breast, and the belly is white. Females and immatures are olive-gray above, whitish below; the wing and tail patches are yellow or yellow-orange.

Voice   Song is variable; usually a rapid series of high, strident notes; frequently alternates between ending notes with rising or falling inflection.

Habitat   Open, deciduous forests and second-growth woodlands.

Range   Breeds from southeastern Alaska to Newfoundland, south to Utah, eastern Oklahoma, the northern Gulf Coast, and South Carolina. Winters from southern Texas and southern Florida to South America.

Ovenbird *Seiurus aurocapillus*

The Ovenbird is a fairly common forest bird in many parts of eastern North America, although there are recent indications that it is being seriously impacted by forest fragmentation and cowbird parasitism. The common name derives from the curious construction of the nest, which is placed on the ground, arched over with dry leaves, and entered from the side—much like an old-fashioned oven. Ovenbirds forage on the ground.

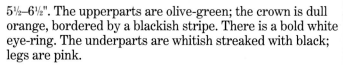

Identification 5½–6½". The upperparts are olive-green; the crown is dull orange, bordered by a blackish stripe. There is a bold white eye-ring. The underparts are whitish streaked with black; legs are pink.

Voice Song is a ringing *teacher-teacher-teacher-teacher*, steadily increasing in volume. Call note is a sharp *tcheek*.

Habitat Deciduous and mixed forests, especially pine-oak.

Range Breeds from northeastern British Columbia to Newfoundland, south to eastern Colorado, northern Arkansas, and northern Georgia. Winters from the Gulf Coast and Florida to South America.

Common Yellowthroat *Geothlypis trichas*

The jaunty song, distinctive black mask, and wrenlike behavior of the male Common Yellowthroat makes it especially winsome. A bird of undergrowth and moist thickets, the yellowthroat is found practically throughout North America. Unlike most wood warblers, which winter in the tropics, Common Yellowthroats regularly winter in moist thickets or near open brooks as far north as New Jersey.

Identification	5–6". Both sexes are greenish brown or olive above with a bright throat and breast, buff-brown flanks, and a dingy white belly. Males have a broad black face mask, bordered above with a bluish-gray band; females and immatures lack the mask.
Voice	Song is a rapid *witchity-witchity-witchity-witchity-wit*. Call note is a husky *tcheck*.
Habitat	Moist thickets, swampy areas, streamsides, and forest clearings.
Range	Breeds throughout most of North America. Winters north to central California and New Jersey.

Scarlet Tanager *Piranga olivacea*

The Scarlet Tanager is one of North America's most striking birds. It belongs to a large family of brilliantly plumaged species largely confined to tropical regions in the Western Hemisphere. Despite its loud and persistent singing and bright coloration, the sluggish, canopy-loving male Scarlet Tanager is often difficult to locate. In fall, the brilliant scarlet coloration of the males is replaced by a dull greenish yellow that is worn until the following spring.

Identification 6½–7½". The adult male is brilliant red with black wings and tail. The female is olive-green above, yellowish below; the wings are dull olive or dusky. The winter male and immatures resemble the female.

Voice Song is a hurried, burry caroling of 4–5 phrases; similar to American Robin's. Call note is an emphatic *chip-burr*, with emphasis on the last syllable.

Habitat Mature deciduous or mixed pine-oak forests, and tall trees in suburban parks.

Range Breeds from southern Manitoba to Maine, south to eastern Oklahoma and northern Georgia. Winters in South America.

Summer Tanager *Piranga rubra*

The Summer Tanager replaces the Scarlet Tanager as a breeding species in the southern United States. In April, the Summer Tanager frequently gets carried north of its normal range by strong southwesterly winds that intercept migrants during their crossing of the Gulf of Mexico from wintering areas in the tropics. Under these circumstances, the weary migrants often show up at birdfeeders in the Northeast.

Identification 7–7¾". The adult male is rosy red with a large, pale bill. The female and immatures are olive-gray above, orange-yellow or mustard below; the bill is sometimes dark in immatures. Males in the first spring are patchy red and yellowish.

Voice Song is a series of clear, sweet, robinlike phrases. Call note is a dry, rapid, and rattled 3-syllabled *pic-kee-tuck.*

Habitat Oak and pine-oak woodlands; in the West, prefers cottonwood-willow riparian forests.

Range Breeds from southeastern California to central Oklahoma; southern Nebraska and southern New Jersey, south to the Gulf Coast. Winters from Mexico to South America.

Northern Cardinal *Cardinalis cardinalis*

Northern Cardinals are among the best-known birds in the United States. Frequent visitors to winter birdfeeders and cheerful songsters in summer, these "red birds" brighten suburban landscapes throughout the year. Like several other southern species, cardinals began a northward range expansion during the 1950s, and they presently breed north to southern Canada.

Identification 8¾–9". The male is bright red with a black face, red crest, and red bill. The female is grayish olive above, buff below; the wings and crest are dull reddish, and the bill is pink. Immatures are like the female but less red.

Voice Song is variable; a loud-whistled *wha-cheeer, wha-cheeer, wha-cheeer,* with the last syllable descending; also a loud, rapid *weeet-weeet-weeet-weeet-weeet.* Call note is a metallic *tsink.*

Habitat Woodland edges, thickets, parks, and gardens.

Range Resident from the Dakotas to Nova Scotia, south to Texas and Florida; also in southern Arizona and New Mexico and southeastern California.

138

Rose-breasted Grosbeak *Pheucticus ludovicianus*

The rich, mellow caroling of the Rose-breasted Grosbeak is a familiar sound in moist woodlands. Both sexes are capable of singing, and the males sing from the nest while incubating. Females often build a second nest while the male is incubating on the first. This way, the birds are able to produce two broods a year.

Identification   7–8". The male has a black head and back, white wing patches, and white underparts with a rose-red patch on the breast; wing linings are pink. The female is streaky brown above, with 2 white wingbars, a brown cheek patch, and a broad white eyebrow stripe; underparts grayish white with brown streaks; wing linings yellow. Bill is large and pale.

Voice   Song is a loud, rich, hurried, and robinlike warble. Call note is a unique *eeek*.

Habitat   Moist, mature woodlands; forest edges; and tall shade trees.

Range   Breeds from Alberta, Ontario, and the Great Lakes to Nova Scotia, south to Kansas and New Jersey; also south in the Appalachians to northern Georgia. Winters from Mexico to South America.

140

Blue Grosbeak *Guiraca caerulea*

Chunky, sluggish, and possessing an oversized, bluish bill, the Blue Grosbeak is typically encountered perched on phone wires or bush tops along roadsides and in field hedgerows. Its blue color, much like that of the Indigo Bunting, often looks black at a distance. Since it feeds heavily on grains and seeds, it is frequently found in weedy fields, unlike most other grosbeaks. When disturbed or upon perching, it twitches its tail in a circular motion.

Identification   6–6¾". The adult male is deep blue with 2 rusty wingbars. The female and immatures are warm brown above, paler below, with 2 prominent buff wingbars and a bluish tinge on the rump. The immature male in the first spring shows a mixture of brown and blue.

Voice   Song is a slow series of sweet, warbled phrases; rises and falls. Call note is a sharp *chink*.

Habitat   Brushy fields, hedgerows, streamside thickets, fence posts.

Range   Breeds from central California, southern Tennessee, and southern New Jersey, south to Texas and central Florida. Winters in Mexico and Central America.

Indigo Bunting *Passerina cyanea*

Though iridescent blue, in some lights an Indigo Bunting may actually look gray or blackish. These birds often sing from a conspicuous perch high in a tree at the edge of a woodland edge. Their lively song can regularly be heard during the heat of a summer's day, well after most other species have stopped singing.

Identification	5½". The male in summer is a deep, brilliant blue; the wings and tail are slightly darker. The female and first winter male are light cinnamon-brown with indistinct breast streaks and faint buff wingbars; the wings and tail have a trace of blue.
Voice	Song is lively and variable, usually comprises several sets of phrases, the last phrase often dropping in pitch: *swee, swee, swee, chew, chew, chew.* Call note is a sharp *chip*.
Habitat	Shrubby woodland edges, power lines, roadsides.
Range	Breeds from southeastern Manitoba to southern New Brunswick, south to central Nebraska; also to central Arizona, Colorado; and central Texas to central Florida. Winters in southern Florida and occasionally along the Gulf Coast; primarily in Central America.

Painted Bunting *Passerina ciris*

Despite the bright colors of the male, the Painted Bunting is shy and often difficult to observe. Although relatively common only in parts of the southeastern United States, Painted Buntings appear with surprising frequency in the Northeast, usually following strong southerly airflows in spring and fall.

Identification 5–5½". The adult male is unmistakable, having a bright blue head, yellow-green back, and greenish-brown wings and tail; the underparts, rump, and eye-ring are bright red. The female and immatures are plain green, usually lighter green or light yellowish below.

Voice Song is a husky or burry warble, like the Warbling Vireo's but higher. Call note is a sharp *chip*.

Habitat Thickets, gardens, suburban parks, and streambanks.

Range Breeds from southeastern New Mexico to southern Missouri and the Gulf Coast; also along the southern Atlantic coast north to central North Carolina. Winters from southeastern Texas, southern Louisiana, and central Florida to Central America.

146

Rufous-sided Towhee *Pipilo erythrophthalmus*

This widespread, oversized sparrow relative is conspicuous as it noisily scratches in the fallen leaves of brushy undergrowth and forest clearings. Being a ground nester of early successional forests, the Rufous-sided Towhee may be declining owing to the steady forest regeneration of previously abandoned brushy pastures.

Identification 7–8½". Eastern males have a black head, throat, and upperparts; the breast and belly are white, bordered by rufous sides and flanks. White spots in the wings and outer tail feathers are obvious in flight. The female is similar, but black areas are replaced by brown. The southeastern population has white instead of red eyes.

Voice Song is typically a trilled *drink-your-tea,* or *deep-blue-sea.* Call note is an up-slurred *to-whee?*

Habitat Forest edges and clearings, brushy areas, pine barrens, and parks with shrubby undergrowth.

Range Breeds from southern British Columbia to Maine, south to Mexico and Florida; absent from much of the Great Plains. Winters throughout the southern two-thirds of the U.S.

American Tree Sparrow *Spizella arborea*

Although it will come to feeders, the American Tree Sparrow prefers fields, overgrown pastures, and brushy river meadows. Undaunted by cold weather, the birds give their sweet and cheery call notes throughout the winter and in early spring, just before they migrate north to Arctic tundra for the summer.

Identification   5½–6½". The head is gray with a bright, rusty cap and eye-line; the back is rusty brown, streaked with black; there are 2 bold, white wingbars. The bill is dark above, yellow below. The underparts are pale gray, the flanks buff; there is a dark spot in the center of the breast.

Voice   Song is a series of sweet, clear whistles; the notes are often doubled. Call note is a musical *teel-a-weet, teel-a-weet;* also *tseeep.*

Habitat   In winter, weedy fields, old pastures, and brushy areas.

Range   Breeds from northern Alaska to northern Quebec, south to northern British Columbia and Labrador. Winters from southern Canada to northern California, central Texas, and South Carolina.

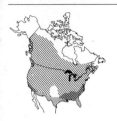

Chipping Sparrow *Spizella passerina*

One of the best-known and most widespread sparrows in North America, the Chipping Sparrow forages on lawns and sidewalks; it is not uncommon to see them feeding the young of Brown-headed Cowbirds, which frequently parasitize their nests. During migration, Chipping Sparrows join flocks of other sparrows in weedy fields and waste areas.

Identification 5–5¾". The adult has a rusty cap, white eyebrows, and a dark line through the eye. The upperparts are brown, streaked with black, and there are 2 white wingbars. The underparts, rump, cheek, and hind neck are gray.

Voice Song is a dry, rapid, unmusical trill, delivered all on one pitch. Call note is a high, sweet *tseep*.

Habitat Forest edges, clearings, parks, and residential areas.

Range Breeds from the Yukon to Newfoundland, south to southern Arizona, New Mexico, southern Texas, the Gulf Coast, and northwestern Florida. Winters from southern California, southern Texas, and Maryland southward; casually north to Oregon, the Great Lakes, and New England.

152

Song Sparrow *Melospiza melodia*

The Song Sparrow is one of the most common songbirds in North America. Although the bird is modest in plumage, its cheery and highly variable song is a characteristic early-spring sound throughout its range. There is wide geographical variation; at least 34 subspecies have been recognized.

Identification 5¾–7". Despite regional variation, most are brown above, streaked with gray and black. The underparts are whitish, heavily streaked with brown; the streaks coalesce to form an irregular dark central spot on the breast. The head shows a broad gray stripe above the eye and a wide dark stripe on each side of the throat.

Voice Song is highly variable; typically begins with several clear notes, *sweet sweet sweet,* followed by a jumbled trill and falling in pitch. Call note is a distinctive *chimp.*

Habitat Thickets, forest edges, marshes, weedy fields, and suburbs.

Range Breeds from southern Alaska to Newfoundland, south to New Mexico and South Carolina. Winters from the southern half of its breeding range to Florida and Mexico.

White-throated Sparrow *Zonotrichia albicollis*

The White-throated Sparrow occurs in more than one color form, with either black and white or black and tan stripes on the crown. Studies show that the birds prefer mates with similar head stripes. In summer, the clear, whistled song of the White-throated Sparrow is a typical sound of northern forests and eastern mountains.

Identification   6½–7¼". The head is boldly striped; yellow spot between the eye and bill; the throat is white. The upperparts are brown, streaked with black; underparts are gray on breast, whitish on belly, and the flanks are washed with olive.

Voice   Song is a plaintive, whistled *sou, wheet, peeverly, peeverly, peeverly.* Call note is a hard *chink;* also a high *tseet.*

Habitat   Coniferous forests with bushy undergrowth, and spruce-fir thickets near mountaintops; residential areas in winter.

Range   Breeds from Mackenzie to Newfoundland, south to central British Columbia, central Michigan, Pennsylvania, and Massachusetts. Winters from northern California to southern New Mexico; and eastern Kansas to Massachusetts, south to central Texas and central Florida.

Dark-eyed Junco *Junco hyemalis*

The Dark-eyed Junco, or "snowbird," is best known as a ground-feeding, winter patron of suburban birdfeeders. Its nervous behavior, flashing white outer tail feathers, and twittering call notes make it easy to distinguish. This species comprises five forms at one time thought to be distinct species. Eastern "Slate-colored" Juncos typically show little contrast between the dark gray of the head and breast and the back and sides.

Identification   5–6½". The upperparts, breast, and sides are slate-gray; the belly and outer tail feathers are white. Both sexes have pink bills; females and immatures have backs and sides washed with buff.

Voice   Song is a loose trill, usually on one pitch. Calls include a rapid twittering, a dull smack, and a *tick* alarm note.

Habitat   Woodlands, fields, and brush; suburban yards in winter.

Range   "Slate-colored" race breeds from Alaska to Newfoundland, south to Manitoba and New England, and south in mountains to Georgia. Winters from southern Canada to Texas and Florida.

158

Bobolink *Dolichonyx oryzivorus*

The explosive and bubbling song of the Bobolink is a familiar summer sound in hay fields and grassy meadows. In late summer, Bobolinks gather into large flocks prior to migrating south. At this season, males assume a plumage resembling that of the females. Because they typically forage in grainfields during migration, Bobolinks are often called "rice birds." Bobolinks winter about as far south in South America as any North American songbird.

Identification   6–8". The breeding male is black with a golden-buff nape and white shoulders and rump. The female, winter male, and immature are buff-yellow with dark streaks on the back, dark stripes on the crown, and a dark eye-line.

Voice   Song is a loud, explosive, and bubbling *Bob-o-link, Bob-o-link, Bob-o-link, Bob-o-link.* Call note is a sharp *pink,* often given in flight.

Habitat   Fields and moist meadows; marshes during migration.

Range   Breeds from southeastern British Columbia to Nova Scotia, south to northern California, the central Great Plains, and New Jersey. Winters in South America.

160

Red-winged Blackbird *Agelaius phoeniceus*

A true harbinger of spring, the Red-winged is gregarious and abundant in wetlands. Owing to a preference for open breeding habitats, the territorial activities of males are easy to observe in early spring. During migration and winter they gather with other blackbirds into staggeringly large flocks and feed on grain. Gulf Coast wintering aggregations may number in the millions.

Identification   7½–9½". The adult male is black with bright red shoulder patches; the folded wing may reveal only the buff-yellow border to the red shoulder patch. The female and juveniles are patterned above and below with dusky brown streaks; they usually show a broad buff eyebrow stripe.

Voice   Song is a liquid *ok-a-lee* or *conk-ka-ree.* Call notes include a sharp, down-slurred *tee-ay;* a low *chuck;* and a metallic *kink.*

Habitat   Marshes, swamps, moist meadows, cornfields and rice fields.

Range   Breeds from southern Alaska, southern Ontario, and Newfoundland south throughout the U.S. Winters in southern two-thirds of U.S. and temperate Northwest.

Eastern Meadowlark *Sturnella magna*

Meadowlarks are birds of open pastures, hay fields, and meadows. Like many grassland birds, they are declining in areas where habitat is being altered through development or the natural succession of forests. Meadowlark nests are extremely difficult to locate because the bird walks to and from the nest site instead of flying directly to it.

Identification 7–10". A starling-shaped bird that flies with alternate flapping and gliding flight. The upperparts are streaked with buff, black, and brown; the head is striped with black and white. The throat and most of underparts are bright yellow; black V on the breast; tail has white outer feathers.

Voice Song is a loud, whistled *see-you, see-year.* Call notes include a dry, buzzy rattle and a buzzy *dzert.*

Habitat Grasslands, farmlands, and meadows; salt marshes during migration and winter.

Range Breeds from southern Manitoba to Nova Scotia, south to Texas and Florida; also in extreme western Texas, New Mexico, and southern Arizona. Winters in all but the northernmost part of its breeding range.

164

Boat-tailed Grackle *Quiscalus major*

The Boat-tailed Grackle is large and long-tailed, and in most areas where it occurs it tends to frequent salt marshes and tidewater situations. In some areas, it also appears in city parks and residential areas, where its bizarre displays and vocalizations cannot fail to attract attention. Once thought to be same species as Great-tailed Grackle of Southwest.

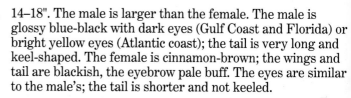

Identification | 14–18". The male is larger than the female. The male is glossy blue-black with dark eyes (Gulf Coast and Florida) or bright yellow eyes (Atlantic coast); the tail is very long and keel-shaped. The female is cinnamon-brown; the wings and tail are blackish, the eyebrow pale buff. The eyes are similar to the male's; the tail is shorter and not keeled.

Voice | A harsh, *jeeb-jeeb-jeeb*; also a sharp *keet-keet-keet* and various whistled notes.

Habitat | Coastal salt marshes, freshwater marshes in Florida, city parks, and residential areas in the Gulf states.

Range | Resident in coastal areas from New York to central Texas and throughout the Florida peninsula; occasionally along rivers inland.

166

Common Grackle *Quiscalus quiscula*

Conspicuous, noisy, and abundant, the Common Grackle is one of the best-known and least-liked birds within its extensive range. During migration and winter, these large birds gather in enormous flocks, sometimes numbering in the millions, to forage in agricultural fields or to roost communally at night with other blackbird species.

Identification   11–13½". The male is larger than the female. The adult is black with an iridescent blue head and purple and bronze tones on the back and wings. The tail is long and wedge-shaped and appears keeled in flight; the eyes are yellow. Juveniles are smoky brown with dark eyes.

Voice   Song is like the opening of a rusty gate: up-slurred *tss-shkleet.* Call note is a harsh *chack.*

Habitat   Mixed woodlands, agricultural fields, wetlands, gardens.

Range   Breeds from northeastern British Columbia to southwestern Newfoundland, south to central Colorado, southern Texas, and Florida. Winters from southern Minnesota and southern New England south to eastern Texas and Florida.

168

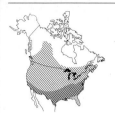

Brown-headed Cowbird *Molothrus ater*

Formerly confined to prairie grasslands where they foraged at the feet of grazing bison, Brown-headed Cowbirds gradually spread eastward as the early colonists cleared the land for agriculture and timber. Today they increasingly represent a threat to eastern songbirds, which they parasitize by laying their eggs in the smaller birds' nests. The foster parents typically end up rearing the young cowbird at the expense of their own young.

Identification 6–8". The adult male is glossy black with a rich brown head; the female is smaller and uniformly brownish gray. Juveniles are pale gray with indistinct streaks below; the immature male shows patches of light gray and glossy black. The bill is thick and finchlike.

Voice Song is squeaky, high-pitched, and bubbly. Female gives a dry chatter.

Habitat Farmlands, fields, open woodlands, and suburbs.

Range Breeds from southern British Columbia, northern Alberta, and Nova Scotia south throughout most of southern Canada and the U.S.

Orchard Oriole *Icterus spurius*

The song of the Orchard Oriole is remarkably similar to that of several other species that often occur in the same habitat. Consequently, in many areas Orchard Orioles are undoubtedly more common than one would suspect. Orchard Orioles often use green grasses in their nests, which quickly become more conspicuous as the grasses turn brown.

Identification 6–7". The adult male has a black hood, upper back, wings, and tail; the lower back, rump, and underparts are deep chestnut. The female is olive-green above, light yellow below, and has 2 white wingbars. The immature male resembles the female but has a black chin and throat.

Voice Song is a rich, hurried, metallic series of warbles and trills, often with down-slurred end note. Call note is soft *chuck*.

Habitat Open country with scattered trees, farmyards, shade trees, and woodland edges.

Range Breeds from southern Manitoba to southern New England, south to eastern New Mexico and northern Florida. Winters from Mexico to South America.

172

Northern Oriole *Icterus galbula*

Throughout much of the eastern United States, male Northern Orioles arrive from the tropics in early May and begin singing and establishing territories almost immediately. The beautifully woven fibrous nests of the birds are constructed on the tips of branches overhanging roadways or streams.

Identification 7–8". The adult male has a black hood, upper back, and wings (with a single white wingbar); the lower back, rump, patches in the tail, and underparts are bright orange. The female is olive to greenish gray above with indistinct streaks on the back; underparts are typically light orange on the breast, yellowish on the belly.

Voice Song is a short series of rich, piping whistles, often disjointed. A loud chatter when alarmed.

Habitat Open deciduous woodlands, forest edges, suburban shade trees, city parks, and residential areas.

Range Eastern race breeds from central Alberta to Nova Scotia, south to Oklahoma and Georgia. Winters primarily from Mexico to northern South America.

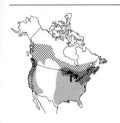

Purple Finch *Carpodacus purpureus*

Primarily a bird of northern coniferous and mixed forests in summer, the Purple Finch regularly attends birdfeeders in winter, although its numbers are highly variable from season to season. Like many northern finches, its winter distribution depends on food availability. First-year males resemble females, giving false impression that females sing.

Identification 5¼–6". The adult male is raspberry-red on the head, back, rump, throat, and breast; the belly and undertail coverts are white; the flanks are indistinctly streaked with brown. Female and immatures are heavily streaked with brown; the bird often appears big-headed.

Voice Song is a rich, bubbly outburst of rapid notes on various pitches; some notes in pairs. Call note is a dry *tic* or *pick*.

Habitat Coniferous and mixed forests, suburbs; feeders in winter.

Range Breeds from British Columbia to Newfoundland, south in the West to southern California; also from the north-central U.S. to the Atlantic coast, south in the Appalachians to Virginia. Winters from southern Canada irregularly south to Mexico and the Gulf Coast.

176

House Finch *Carpodacus mexicanus*

Since its introduction on Long Island, New York, in the 1940s, this western finch has colonized much of the eastern United States. A gregarious visitor at winter feeders and a frequent nester in hanging flower planters and ornamental evergreens, the cheerful House Finch has become commonplace in even the most populated eastern cities. There appears to be a positive correlation between the spread of the House Finch and a decline in House Sparrow numbers.

Identification	5–5½". The male is brownish with the forehead, eyebrow, rump, throat, and breast orange to deep rose-red; the grayish-buff belly and flanks are heavily streaked with brown. The female is similar but lacks red and is distinctly streaked below; there is no conspicuous head pattern.
Voice	Song is a burry, canary-like warble, usually ending with an ascending *zeeee.* Call note is a hard chirp.
Habitat	Cities and residential areas; also weedy fields and coastal dunes in fall.
Range	In the East, resident from Michigan to Maine, south to Georgia.

178

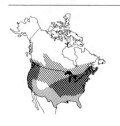

American Goldfinch *Carduelis tristis*

A regular patron of thistle-seed feeders throughout the year, the American Goldfinch lends color and sound wherever it appears. Its lively song and animated aerial territorial displays make it especially conspicuous in late spring; however, its propensity for using thistledown in its nests makes it one of the latest songbirds to nest.

Identification	4½–5". The breeding male is bright yellow with a black crown, wings, and tail; the rump and wingbars are white. The female and nonbreeding male are olive-brown above and buff-gray below; the wings and tail are black, wingbars white. Birds usually show a trace of yellow at any season.
Voice	Song is a jumble of sweet, twittering notes. Flight note is a sweet *per-chick-o-ree;* also a plaintive *chi-ee.*
Habitat	Thickets, overgrown pastures, marshy areas, weedy grasslands, and suburban parks and yards.
Range	Breeds from southern British Columbia and northern Alberta to Newfoundland, south to southern California, Utah, Nebraska, Oklahoma, and South Carolina. Winters throughout most of its breeding range south to Mexico.

180

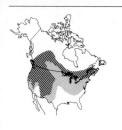

Evening Grosbeak *Coccothraustes vespertinus*

Although somewhat unpredictable in their winter movements, Evening Grosbeaks sometimes gather in great flocks southward as far as the southern United States. In summer, they concentrate in northern coniferous areas, often for spruce budworm outbreaks. Originally a western species that began colonizing eastern forests in early 1900s.

Identification 7–8". A robust bird with an enormous, greenish-yellow, conical bill. The male has a yellow forehead and eyebrow; the head, upper back, and breast are rich brown. The lower back, rump, and belly are bright yellow; wings are black with large white patches. Female is grayer, yellow below.

Voice Song is a disconnected warble. Call note is a loud *cleep* or *cleer*; also a soft clicking note, especially in flight.

Habitat In the East, mainly northern coniferous and mixed forests; irregularly at suburban birdfeeders in winter.

Range Breeds from British Columbia to Nova Scotia, south throughout western mountains; also to Minnesota, northern New York, and northern New England. Winters from southern Canada irregularly south to the southern U.S.

182

House Sparrow *Passer domesticus*

Along with the European Starling, the House Sparrow is perhaps the most successful passerine species in urban North America. House Sparrows were introduced into this country in the mid-1800s for the purpose of controlling noxious insect pests. Their population quickly increased, and soon the birds became agricultural pests themselves. With the decline of agriculture and horse transportation, reduced available grain caused the number of sparrows to decline. Nevertheless, House Sparrows continue to threaten the successful nesting of Purple Martins and bluebirds.

Identification 5½–6½". The male is brown above, streaked with black; there is a single bold white wingbar. The head has a gray crown, chestnut nape, and grayish-white cheek. The throat and breast are black; the rest of the underparts are gray. The female and immatures are plainer, with a brown crown, buff stripe behind the eye, and grayish-tan underparts.

Voice Various twitters and a repeated *chirp, cheep.*

Habitat Farmlands, cities, towns, and suburban areas.

Range Throughout most of southern Canada and the entire U.S.

184

Parts of a Bird

eye-ring

eye line

ear patch

nape

back

tertials

secondaries

rump

primaries

tail feathers

undertail coverts

crown with median
crown stripe

eyebrow

lore

throat

breast

wingbars

flank

belly

Glossary

Coverts
The small feathers covering bases of usually larger feathers, providing a smooth, aerodynamic surface.

Crown
The uppermost surface of the head.

Eyebrow
A stripe running horizontally from base of bill above the eye.

Eye line
A stripe running horizontally from base of bill through the eye.

Eye-ring
A fleshy or feathered ring around the eye.

Lore
The area between base of bill and the eye.

Mandible
One of the two parts, upper and lower, of a bird's bill.

Morph (color phase)
One of two or more distinct color types within the same species and occurring independently of age, sex, or season.

Nape
The back of the head, including the hindneck.

Polymorphic
Having two or more morphs or phases within a single species.

Primaries
The longest and outermost (usually 9 or 10) flight feathers.

Race (subspecies)
A geographical population that is slightly different from other populations of the same species.

Rump
The lower back, just above the tail.

Secondaries
The inner flight feathers that are attached to the "forearm."

Tertials
The three innermost secondaries closest to the body.

Wing bar
A bar of contrasting color on the upper wing coverts.

Index

Credits

Photographers

Ron Austing (24–25, 41, 45, 47, 51, 99, 121, 165)
Nick Bergkessel (105)
Gay Bumgarner (143)
Sharon Cummings (149, 163)
Rob Curtis/The Early Birder (71, 73, 87, 91, 97, 135, 155)

DEMBINSKY PHOTO ASSOCIATES:
Sharon Cummings (169)
John Gerlach (159)
Adam Jones (147)
Doug Locke (85)
Skip Moody (83)
Carl R. Sams (35, 161)
George E. Stewart (181)

Jack Dermid (57)
Larry R. Ditto (37)
Michael H. Francis (167)
John Heidecker/Nature Photos (59)
Kevin T. Karlson (39, 61, 65)
Harold Lindstrom (95, 145, 153, 173, 185)

Barry W. Mansell (49)
Joe McDonald (67, 103)
C. Allan Morgan (137)
Arthur & Elaine Morris/Birds As Art (33, 63, 101, 117, 133, 157)

PHOTO/NATS, INC.:
Priscilla Connell (109)
Sam Fried (179)
Ed Thurston (175)

Rod Planck (183)
Jean Pollock (43)
James H. Robinson (131)
Johann Schumacher Design (3, 111, 113, 127)
Ervio Sian (119)
Rob & Ann Simpson (53, 123, 171)
Brian E. Small (129)
Hugh P. Smith, Jr. (31, 115)
Tom J. Ulrich (29, 69, 93, 141, 177)
Mark F. Wallner (125, 151)
Larry West (55, 79, 81, 89, 107, 139)
Paul Zimmerman (27)
Tim Zurowski (Front Cover, 75, 77)

Cover photograph: Purple Finch by Tim Zurowski

Title page: Yellow Warbler by Rob & Ann Simpson

Spread (24–25): Indigo Bunting by Ron Austing

Illustrators

Range maps by Paul Singer
Drawings by Barry Van Dusen (186–187)
Silhouette drawings by Douglas Pratt and Paul Singer

Staff for this book

Publisher: Andrew Stewart
Managing Editor: Edie Locke
Production Manager:
Dierdre Duggan Ventry
Assistant to the Publisher:
Kelly Beekman
Text Editor: Carole Berglie
Consultant: John Farrand, Jr.
Photo Editor: Lori J. Hogan
Designer: Sheila Ross

Original series design by
Massimo Vignelli

All editorial inquiries on this title
should be addressed to:
Pocket Guides
P.O. Box 479
Woodstock, VT 05091
editors@thefieldguideproject.com

To purchase this book or other
National Audubon Society
illustrated nature books, please
contact:
Alfred A. Knopf, Inc.
1745 Broadway
New York, NY 10019
(800) 733-3000
www.randomhouse.com

NATIONAL AUDUBON SOCIETY® POCKET GUIDE

NATIONAL AUDUBON SOCIETY

The mission of NATIONAL AUDUBON SOCIETY *is to conserve and restore natural ecosystems, focusing on birds, other wildlife, and their habitats for the benefit of humanity and the earth's biological diversity.*

One of the largest environmental organizations, AUDUBON has 550,000 members, 100 sanctuaries and nature centers, and 508 chapters in the Americas, plus a professional staff of scientists, educators, and policy analysts.

The award-winning *Audubon* magazine, sent to all members, carries outstanding articles and color photography on wildlife, nature, the environment, and conservation. Audubon also publishes *Audubon Adventures*, a children's newspaper reaching 450,000 students. Audubon offers nature education for teachers, families, and children through ecology camps and workshops in Maine, Connecticut, and Wyoming, plus unique, traveling undergraduate and graduate degree programs through *Audubon Expedition Institute*.

AUDUBON sponsors books, on-line nature activities, and travel programs to exotic places like Antarctica, Africa, Australia, Baja California, and the Galápagos Islands. For information about how to become an Audubon member, to subscribe to *Audubon Adventures*, or to learn more about our camps and workshops, please contact:

AUDUBON
225 Varick Street, 7th Floor
New York, NY 10014
(212) 979-3000 or (800) 274-4201
www.audubon.org